The Process Server's Handbook
by
Kenneth Brennan

No part may be duplicated or distributed
without express written permission from the author.

Copyright 2010

Table of Contents:

Forward   3

Chapter I   5
Introduction to Civil Procedure and Service of Process.
Civil vs. Criminal Law * Procedural Law * Service of Process Licensing Pros and Cons * Officer of the Court?

Chapter II   12
Forms and Orders
Glossary of Terms * Subpoena * Summons * Restraining order Return of Service * Affidavit of Service

Chapter III   25
General Rules of Process Service
Personal Service * Substituted Service * Service by Mail, Publication, Voluntary acceptance * Serve or post * Affidavit of mailing * Affidavit of due diligence * Trespassing * Deadlines * Dies non juridicum.

Chapter IV   34
Federal Rules of Civil Procedure
Test your knowledge

Chapter V   44
Serving Process
Modes of Personal Service * Difficult Individuals * Interviewing Neighbors * Attitude and demeanor * Keeping a journal * Due Diligence Uniform & Dress * Supplies, ID and Badges * Firearms and other weapons * Projecting a professional image.

Chapter VI   65
The Business of Process Service
Soliciting Business * Incorporation * Insurance & Bond * Professional Associations * Support services *Specialties & sidelines

Forward

My first job as a process server was nearly 20 years ago working for a local law firm where my fiancée was employed. I got the job by chance. I was literally in the right place at the right time. As I waited at the reception desk for my betrothed to break for lunch, the receptionist asked me if I could deliver some documents to a nearly business that afternoon. She offered me $10.00. Big money for a kid fresh out of high school with no prospects for employment. Knowing nothing about what I was doing, I took the challenge and that led to a nice part-time job as a private process server.

Many years later, I decided to get back into the business, part-time, to make ends meet. Unfortunately, I found it to be much more complicated than I had previously thought. The industry had changed a great deal and gaining work as a private server was a rare opportunity often delegated to friends and colleagues. In other words, its all about who you know. Undeterred, I decided to start my own firm and hire employees to do the soliciting and serving for me.

Looking back on my first experiences as a process server I realized that it was to my best interest to train my employees before sending them out on the streets. The first thing I did was search for an existing process server training course. What I found was disturbing. There were only two "training courses" available and neither were in any way reputable. One was deceptively vague and decades out-of-date, the other was a snake-oil scam intended only to get you to part with your money in exchange for "inside secrets" which were never delivered. Both "courses" marketed themselves by promising a get-rich-quick approach to the business of Process Serving.

It became immediately clear that I needed to develop my own training course in order to ensure reliable and productive employees.

After several months of research, I developed a comprehensive training program specifically for my state of operations (Pennsylvania) This allowed me to train potential employees fast so that they could quickly become productive. Later, I developed that training into a correspondence course for the public. My motivation was to provide better information than was currently available. This book is derived from that course.

Process serving can be a fun and lucrative occupation. Like any business, it involves a degree of risk. The amount of money that one can make as a process server varies and depends on many factors including; the local market, legal culture and the investment of your personal resources. Unlike the typical business endeavor, the failure of process servers to comply with local and federal laws can have serious repercussions. To achieve success in the business of process service one must be diligent in compliance with the law and also exercise a successful business strategy. It is the purpose of this course to educate and prepare new process servers to be successful in both respects.

Disclaimer

Every effort has been made to ensure the information contained in this course is accurate and up to date. However, you are ultimately responsible for compliance with the laws of the jurisdiction in which you operate. Neither authors or publishers of this course assume any responsibility for errors, omissions or misinterpretation of the information contained herein. Proper and legal use of this information is your own responsibility. Throughout this book you will be reminded to check and conform to local and federal laws.

Chapter I

Introduction to Civil Procedure and Service of Process

Civil vs. Criminal Law

The US judicial system is essentially divided into two types of legal procedure: Civil and Criminal. Civil trials concern the resolution of claims by an individual or party against another individual or party. Civil trials are to be distinguished from "criminal trials," in which the state prosecutes an individual for violation of criminal law. Civil trials can be used by anyone to enforce, redress, or protect their legal rights through court orders and monetary awards. The two types of trials, civil and criminal, are very different in character and thus have separate procedural rules and practices.

In the United States, the federal courts follow the *Federal Rules of Civil Procedure*. State courts follow their own state rules of civil procedure, which are modeled closely on the Federal rules.

Civil procedure may be defined as the rules by which courts conduct civil trials.

Procedural Law

Procedural law is distinguished from *Substantive Law*, which creates, defines, and regulates the rights and duties of individuals. Procedural law prescribes the methods by which individuals may enforce substantive laws. The basic concern of procedural law is the fair, orderly, efficient, and predictable application of substantive laws. Procedural guidance can be found in court rules, statutes, and judicial decisions.

Substantive law refers to the body of rules that determine the rights and obligations of individuals and collective bodies.

Procedural law is the body of legal rules that govern the process for determining the rights of parties.

Service of Process

Service of process is the procedure employed to give legal notice to a person (such as a defendant) of a legal action involving them. The purpose of service of process is to give the served party the opportunity to respond. Usually, such notice involves a set of court documents, called "*Process*".

Legal Process Servers are individuals who serve (deliver) these legal documents on behalf of the court. Proper execution of service is critical to a sound legal case. In order to effect proper service on an individual or business entity, process servers often perform many of the same duties performed by a private investigator; including surveillance and locating individuals who do not wish to be served.

The term "Process" as in "Process Server" comes from the legal principles of *Due Process* and *Procedure* which refer to requirement that a defendant be given notice, in a specific way, of legal action against or involving him. Because the court system relies on the service of due process to move forward, the Process Server, therefore, is a necessary cog in the machinery of the legal system.

Initial responsibility of service traditionally falls upon local public officials of the jurisdiction to which a lawsuit pertains, such as the Sheriff, Constable or a Deputy thereof; however, in Civil proceedings, most states permit a private citizen to serve particular types of process. These, non-official process servers are called *Special Process Servers* or *Specials.* All private process servers who are not elected or appointed government officials are considered special process servers. In general, special process servers are independent contractors hired by attorneys or parties to a lawsuit to serve legal documents (process) on behalf of the courts. This book addresses the role and duties of special servers.

There are many reasons for the use of special servers. First, the resources of local officials are usually limited. Most metropolitan areas can generate hundreds of papers per day. Therefore, depending on local regulations, the Sheriff and/or constable may serve a particular variety of document, usually related to crime and domestic relations, thereby leaving other varieties of civil process for special servers. (The types of process you will handle will depend on the laws of the state(s) win which you operate)

In addition, public officials are often restricted to their own jurisdiction. A sheriff who needs to make service in an adjacent county may not be allowed to do so. In most cases there are remedies for this. For example; a sheriff of one county can be deputized by the sheriff of another county in which he is to make service. This, however, takes additional time and resources. The special process server, as a citizen, enjoys far more freedom in this regard. Under most circumstances the special server may cross county and state borders at will.

Licensing Pros and Cons

A few states require Process Servers to be licensed or registered, often through the office of the sheriff or other responsible government agency. These are called *Regulated States*. Exactly what defines *Registration*, as opposed to, *License*, depends on the specific state and/or jurisdiction. The main difference is that licensing will usually require a specific standard of qualification, often through established training and exam; whereas registration, itself, may be the only requirement to work as a special process server.

We have found that the limited scope of most State and City licensing courses tend to tell you what you "need to know" in order to be "approved". But they often don't provide actual skills you will need to do your job well or to operate outside the jurisdiction for which they are licensing you. Further, they don't address the business aspect of process service. In unregulated states you are mostly on your own when it comes to training and breaking into the business. Again, this book should help you with both.

Some regulated states grant special privileges to process servers, such as the right to trespass in order to make service, or the privilege to carry a firearm in the service of one's duty. Any such privileges depend on the rules of each state and jurisdiction.

It is easy to determine whether your state is regulated by visiting your state website and reading the civil rules of service. You should periodically double-check your state's current rules in case there have been changes.

There are pros and cons to living in both regulated and unregulated states. While in unregulated states a process server is free to just go ahead and set up shop, it is often much harder to break into the business than in regulated states. That is because, in unregulated states, there tend to be business monopolies on process service which can make it harder for newcomers to generate new clients.

In Regulated states there are usually official lists of approved process servers. In theory, this list is consulted every time an attorney needs a special server. Therefore, it may actually be easier to get work in a regulated state; however, just as in unregulated states, the larger paper-brokers tend to hold monopolies.

Finally; most, if not all, regulated states require you to secure a bond and/or insurance. In states that do not *License* but require *Registration*, securing a bond is the primary qualification to become Registered. Even if you are in an unregulated state you should still have this sort of protection. Often, your clients will require it. At the least, it could help a potential client select you over another uninsured and non-bonded server. More on this later.

Officer of the Court?

The term *Officer of the court* can be applied to all those who, in some degree, have a legal part in the functioning of the judicial system. There is much confusion about whether the *Special Process Server* is considered an *Officer of the court*. In some jurisdictions, particularly in regulated states and cities, special process servers may be specifically appointed by the court for the purpose of making service. In this situation they become "*Officers of the court*" in regard to that particular case. However, in unregulated states, the majority of work a special server can expect to handle does not require him to be appointed by the court, therefore, his status as an Officer of the court, may be ambiguous. Generally Speaking, whenever a special process server is **specifically named and appointed by the court** to serve process, he becomes an "Officer of the court". But what does this mean?

Appointment as court officer may, or may not, bestow special powers, rights or protections to the server. These privileges vary from state-to-state and even city-to-city; however; some rights and privileges of special process servers are nearly universal. For example; in most jurisdictions it is unlawful to interfere with the duty of a process server under penalty of law; regardless of their status as an *officer of the court*. In addition, special process servers are generally allowed to conduct investigation and surveillance of individuals for the purpose of service.

In practice; whether or not a process server qualifies as an officer of the court is irrelevant. The real issue is whether it is lawful for the special server to identify himself as such. As a rule; when in doubt, Don't! It really does not matter whether or not you hold Court Officer status. Your role as a process server provides enough authority to perform your duty in an effective and lawful manner.

Unless the rules of your jurisdiction specifically address the matter, it is best to never identify yourself as an "Officer of the court". These three little words can have disastrous results if it can be claimed that you have impersonated law enforcement. It is always best to simply identify oneself as a Process Sever for the specific Court you represent. It may seem trivial, but it is best practice not to take chances where ambiguous legal terminology is concerned.

Here is an example: Say you are dispatched to serve a Subpoena issued by the Clerk of Courts[1] upon a Mr. Spencer; an office manager in a busy business-center. You approach the receptionist at the desk and politely state that you must personally give some legal documents to Mr. Spencer.

It is not uncommon to meet resistance in this sort of situation because it is the receptionist's job to filter access to Mr. Spencer. The receptionist may ask you if you have an appointment and when you say no, Mr. Spencer may become "unavailable'. At this time you would explain your role as a process server and that you have important time-sensitive legal documents to deliver to Mr. Spencer. The receptionist may offer to take the papers for you but you are **required** to execute personal service on Mr. Spencer; which you explain to the receptionist.

---

1 In the United States federal courts, each district court, court of appeals, and bankruptcy court, as well as the Supreme Court, has its own clerk, appointed by the judges of the court. The clerk is the custodian of the court's records and also has responsibility for collecting fees and other deposits of money made with the court. The court clerk is not to be confused with the law clerk who assists the judge in making legal determinations. And in the courts within the City of New York, the Court Clerk, who is a Peace Officer, is the highest ranking, non-judicial person in the courtroom. The Court Clerk is the supervisor of the Court Officers in the Courtroom.

The next step would be to inquire as to when Mr. Spencer will be available to receive these documents and then offer to wait. This is only fair. If, however, you feel that you are simply being put-off or ignored, you may discretely, but authoritatively, state something to the effect of, "*I have been charged with the service of legal process on Mr. Spencer on behalf of the (specific) Court. It would be in his best interest to receive these papers as soon as possible.*" This should do the trick, but just in case it does not, we will revisit this scenario in another chapter.

What is most important is that you do not misrepresent your authority when attempting to make service. Since this scenario involves a Subpoena issued by the Clerk of Courts, the document was probably drafted from a blank by an attorney in which case it does not require special *appointment* of a process server. Therefore, you are NOT an *Officer of the Court* and should not represent yourself as such.

Chapter II
Forms and orders

The following are definitions of terms relating to the Summons and Subpoena:

Affidavit: An affidavit is a formal sworn statement of fact, signed by the author, who is called the affiant or deponent, and witnessed as to the authenticity of the affiant's signature by a taker of oaths, such as a notary public or commissioner of oaths. The name is medieval Latin for "he has declared upon oath". An affidavit is a type of verified statement which serves as legal evidence.

Uses of affidavits include:
- To allow evidence to be gathered from witnesses or participants who may not be available to testify in person before the court, or who may otherwise fear for their safety if their true identities are revealed in court.
- To obtain a declaration on a legal document, such as an application for voter registration, that the information provided by the applicant is truthful to the best of the applicant's knowledge. If, after signing such a declaration, the information is found to be deliberately untrue with the intent to deceive, the applicant may face perjury charges.

Affidavits may be written in the first or third person, depending on who drafted the document. If in the first person, the document's component parts are:
- a commencement which identifies the affiant;
- the individual averments, almost always numbered as mandated by law, each one making a separate claim;
- a statement of truth generally stating that everything is true, under penalty of perjury, fine, or imprisonment; and
- an attestation clause, usually a jurat, at the end certifying the affiant made oath and the date.

If an affidavit is notarized or authenticated, it will also include a caption with a venue and title in reference to judicial proceedings. In some cases, an introductory clause, called a preamble, is added attesting that the affiant personally appeared before the authenticating authority.

An Affidavit must be signed in the presence of the Notary Public who administers the oath. We will further explore a type of affidavit most often used by process servers later in this chapter.

Complaint: A complaint is the first pleading filed by a plaintiff which initiates a lawsuit. A complaint sets forth the relevant allegations of fact that give rise to one or more legal causes of action along with a *prayer for relief*. In some situations, a complaint is called a petition, in which case the party filing it is called the petitioner and the other party is the respondent.

Motion: A legal motion is a procedural device in law to bring a limited, contested issue before a court for decision. A motion may be thought of as a request to the judge (or judges) to make a decision about the case. Motions may be made at any point in administrative, criminal or civil proceedings, although that right is regulated by court rules which vary from place to place. The party requesting the motion may be called the movant, or may simply be the moving party. The party opposing the motion is the nonmovant or nonmoving party.

Non-est: If, after exercising due diligence, you are unable to locate, or otherwise effect service upon an individual, you must file a return of no service. (non Est) Most documents have a check box for non-est returns. In addition, you will file an affidavit of due diligence (covered later) to show that you exercised adequate effort before giving up.

Party: An individual, group or organization involved in a law suit.

Petition: A petition can also be the title of a legal pleading that initiates a case to be heard before a court. The initial pleading in a civil lawsuit that seeks only money (damages) might be titled (in most U.S. courts) a complaint; an initial pleading in a lawsuit seeking non-monetary or "equitable" relief such as a request for a writ of mandamus or habeas corpus, or for custody of a child or for probate of a will, would instead be termed a petition.

Prayer for Relief: A part of a complaint in which the plaintiff describes the remedies that the plaintiff seeks from the court. For example, the plaintiff may ask for an award of compensatory damages, punitive damages, attorney's fees, an injunction to make the defendant stop a certain activity, or all of these. The request for a specific amount of money may be referred to as an *ad damnum clause*.

Writ: In common law, a writ is a formal written order issued by a body with administrative or judicial jurisdiction; in modern usage, this body is generally a court. Warrants, prerogative writs and subpoenas are types of writs; there are many others.

The Subpoena

A subpoena (pronounced (Sub-Pina) commands the presence of a witness to testify, "under a penalty for failure"; meaning that failure to comply with the orders of the Subpoena will resulting legal ramifications. The term Subpoena is Latin for "Under Penalty".

Blank subpoenas are usually issued, by the *clerk of the court*, to Lawyers who fill them out as needed. It is the responsibility of the lawyer representing the plaintiff or defendant to serve the subpoena on the witness; via a process server. This is the type of Subpoena most commonly handled by Special servers. The subpoena will usually be on the letterhead of the court where the case is filed and will name the parties to the case.

There are generally two types of Subpoena. These include subpoena duces tecum and subpoena ad testificandum.

A **subpoena duces tecum** (Latin for "bring with you under penalty of punishment") is also called a records-only subpoena. It requires the parties named to appear and produce tangible evidence or documents for use at a hearing or trial.

A **subpoena ad testificandum** (Latin for "summons to testify orally") is an order requiring a party to appear in person and provide oral testimony for use at a hearing or trial.

Sample: **SUBPOENA DUCES TECUM**

NAME OF ATTORNEY
ADDRESS OF ATTORNEY
PHONE:

BEFORE THE DIVISION OF OCCUPATIONAL AND PROFESSIONAL LICENSING. DEPARTMENT OF COMMERCE, STATE OF UTAH.

JOHN DOE,

Petitioner,

SUBPOENA DUCES TECUM

vs.

RICHARD ROE, M.D.

Respondent.

Case No. _____

TO: JOHN Doe.

000 Medical Plaza

Anytown, U.S.A. 00000

RE: John Doe

Date of Birth: 08/28/48

YOU ARE COMMANDED to produce at the offices of (Name), (Address), on or before (Date), a complete copy of your medical records, pertaining to the above-referenced individual who has requested the Division of Occupational and Professional Licensing, to conduct a prelitigation panel review of a claim of medical malpractice. Attendance is not required if records are timely forwarded to the indicated address.

DATED this _____ day of _____, 20__.

By: _____

James Doe, Prelitigation Supervisor
Division of Occupational & Professional Licensing

At the top of the Civil Subpoena appears the case number, hearing date and time, name and address of the issuing court, and named parties in the form of Plaintiff vs. Defendant or Party in regards to a complaint or petition.

On all court orders, including the subpoena, the date of the hearing is significant because it determines your deadline to make service. Every jurisdiction has a time-limit for the execution of service that is based on the hearing date. Common limits are 14 to 30 days before the day of the hearing. In some cases, you may even have up until the very hour of the hearing to make service. It is critical that you understand and monitor such deadlines per the rules of the jurisdiction in which the order originates. To determine a deadline for service, simply count count backward from the hearing date. That is your service deadline. Never confuse the hearing date with the date the document was issued, or the deadline for service. If the documents do not state the time-frame for service check with the rules of your jurisdiction and those of the document's origin.

The Summons

A Summons notifies a defendant that a law suit has been filed against him and that he is required to respond within a specific period of time. The summons announces a date by which the defendant(s) must either appear in court, or respond in writing to the court or the opposing party or parties.

A summons will contain the language "You are hereby commanded to report in person to the clerk of this court" or similar, describing the specific location, scheduled date and time of the appearance. Some issuing jurisdictions include an admonishment advising the subject of the criminal penalty for failure to comply with a subpoena, and reminding him or her not to leave the court facilities until excused by a competent authority. In some situations the person is paid.

Unlike the Subpoena which is drafted by an Attorney, the Summons is issued by the directly by the court. With the Summons will be attached a complaint, petition, motion, writ or other pleading.

Sample: **SUMMONS**

IN THE COURT OF COMMONS PLEAS FOR THE STATE OF
DELAWARE IN AND FOR _____ COUNTY _____

Civil Action No._____

Name (s)

Plaintiff (s), _____

   vs.

Defendant (s)._____

TO THE SHERIFF OF_____ COUNTY, YOU ARE COMMANDED:

To Summon the above named defendant(s) and serve upon said defendant(s) a copy of this summons and complaint.

TO THE ABOVE NAMED DEFENDANT(S):

Within twenty (20) days after you receive this Summons, excluding the day you receive it, you must file an Answer to the attached Complaint if you want to deny the allegations. The original of your Answer must be filed with the Clerk's Office of the Court of Common Pleas,

_____, Delaware and must include proof that a copy of the Answer was served on the plaintiff or his/her attorney who is named on this Summons.

Failure to file an Answer denying the allegations will result in a judgment against you, and action may be taken by the plaintiff or his/her attorney to satisfy the judgment.

DATED: _____   _____
                                                                                     Clerk

Name of Plaintiff/Plaintiff's Attorney

Address

Telephone Number

The Restraining Order

Another form of process sometimes handled by private servers is the restraining order. A restraining order is a form of legal injunction. The term is most commonly used in reference to domestic violence, harassment, stalking or sexual assault. Each state has some form of domestic violence restraining order law and many states also have specific restraining order laws for stalking and sexual assault. In most unlicensed jurisdictions, due to the potential for criminal charges, law enforcement and public officials usually serve restraining orders.

The Return of Service

Once any service of process has been effected, the responsible officer or process server must typically file a return of service, also called a "Sheriffs return", with with the court (or provide one to the plaintiff to file with the court). The return of service indicates the time and place at which service was effected, the person served, and any additional information needed to establish that service was properly made. It is signed by the process server, and operates as prima facie evidence that service of process was effectively made.

Depending on the jurisdiction, the Sheriffs Return may be included as part of the summons; usually on the bottom or on the reverse side. It is becoming more common for the return to provide a space specifically for the signature of Special servers; in which case you will fill it out accordingly. Otherwise you may fill out the portion addressed to "Sheriff".

Sample: **RETURN OF SERVICE**

I, _____ , certify that I this day summoned

the within named _____

to appear and give evidence at Court as directed by the attached

subpoena by delivering

___ in hand, (or) ___ leaving at _____ (Address) _____
a copy of the subpoena together with _____ fees

for attendance and travel.

I further certify that I am not a party to the above entitled action

and that 1 am not less than 18 years of age.

Signed under penalties of perjury this _____ day of _____ , in

the year ___

before a Notary Public _____

Sign and Seal

(Note: The Return, itself, may not require notarization.)

Affidavit of Service

In addition to the Sheriffs Return, or Return of Service, it is often necessary for private servers (Specials) and any unofficial server to also complete an *Affidavit of Service*. The affidavit is separate from the Sheriffs return and it must be notarized.

The Affidavit of Service is your sworn testimony that you made service; or that you practiced *due diligence* in attempt to serve. Some states and jurisdictions have begun to combine the Sheriffs Return with the Affidavit of Service on a single form that is part of the Subpoena or Summons itself.

When you pick up a subpoena from an attorney it will include at least two copies. One is to be served to the named party and other will accompany the Affidavit of Service to be filed with the court.

Before filing the return and affidavit with the court, you must have the affidavit notarized by a Notary Public. Essentially, the Notary administers your sworn statement of the facts noted in your affidavit. This document will become a record of the court.

Failure to file an affidavit of service does not necessarily invalidate the actual service of process. Your personal testimony, or even your journal, can provide such evidence but it is far less bothersome to avoid being summoned to court altogether. Simply remember to always file your affidavit of service with the court. Attach it to an original copy of the subpoena, summons etc. Besides; failing to file a "return" (including the affidavit) just may result in never being called by that attorney again. See Attachment: Affidavit of Service.

Remember, an affidavit must be signed before the Notary Public who administers the oath. Signing a affidavit of service before you bring it to the Notary will result in its rejection. You will also need to bring an ID with you to the Notary's office.

Sample: **AFFIDAVIT OF SERVICE** 1 of 3

(NAME OF COURT)

PLAINTIFF/PETITIONER _____

VS

DEFENDANT/RESPONDENT _____

CASE NUMBER _____

I_____ , being first duly sworn, **depose and** say: that I am over the age of 18 years and not a party to this action, and that within the boundaries of **the state where service** was **effected**, I was authorized by law to perform said service.

I served _____
   NAME OF PERSON / ENTITY BEING SERVED

with (list documents)_____

by leaving with_____
       NAME   RELATIONSHIP

At __ **Residence**

ADDRESS _____ CITY _____ STATE _____

__ **Business**

ADDRESS _____ CITY _____ STATE _____

On_____AT _____
       DATE   TIME

___ Inquired if subject was a member of the U.S. Military and was informed they are not.

Thereafter copies of the documents were mailed by prepaid, first class mail on_____ from _____
     DAY   CITY   STATE   ZIP

Sample: AFFIDAVIT OF SERVICE 2 of 3

Manner of Service:

___ **Personal:** By personally delivering copies to the person being served.

___ **Substituted at Residence:** By leaving copies at the dwelling house or usual place of abode of the person being

served with a member of the household over the age of_____ and explaining the general nature of the papers.

___ **Substituted at Business:** By leaving, during office hours, copies at the office of the person/entity being served with

the person apparently in charge thereof.

___ **Posting:** By posting copies in a conspicuous manner to the front door of the person/entity being served.

___ **Non-Est:** (Non-Service) After due search, careful inquiry and diligent attempts at the address(es) listed above, I have been unable to effect process upon the person/entity being served because of the following reason(s):

___ **Unknown at Address.**

___ **Moved, Left no Forwarding.**

___ **Service Canceled by Litigant.**

___ **Unable to Serve In Timely Fashion.**

___ **Address Does Not Exist.**

___ **Other** _____

Sample: AFFIDAVIT OF SERVICE 3 of 3

Service Attempts: Service was attempted on:

(1) ___/___/___ ___:___   (2) ___/___/___ ___:___
      DATE   TIME   DATE   TIME

(3) ___/___/___ ___:___   (4) ___/___/___ ___:___
      DATE   TIME   DATE   TIME

(5) ___/___/___ ___:___   (6) ___/___/___ ___:___
      DATE   TIME   DATE   TIME

Description:. Age____ Sex____ Race____ Height_____ Weight_____ Hair____ Beard____ Glasses____

-----------------Notary-----------------

SIGNATURE OF PROCESS SERVER:
_____

SUBSCRIBED AND SWORN to before me
this_____ day of _____, 20___ , by_____
Proved to me on the basis of satisfactory evidence to be the person(s) who appeared before me.

SIGNATURE OF NOTARY PUBLIC.
_____

NOTARY PUBLIC for the state of. _____

SEAL: _____

Chapter III

General Rules of Process Service

In the past, people did not have the right to know that there were legal proceedings against them. In some cases, they would only find out when authorities arrived to seized their property, sometimes throwing them into debtor's prison until their debts were paid. The fifth and fourteenth amendments to the United States Constitution prohibit the federal and state governments from depriving any person of life, liberty or property without due process of law. Therefore the process server is "serving" the recipient with notice of their constitutional right to due process of the law.

All states have laws that govern the way service of process is effected. Stipulations include licensing requirements, forms, deadlines and differences in the process of service upon individuals, government officials and corporations.

There are also specific procedures and rules for different courts, from local small claims courts to United States district courts. Failure to follow these guidelines may deem the attempted service improper. It is not uncommon for a defendant to claim that he was not served process. This defense is too often effective because service of process upon defendant did not follow legal procedure. In other words, the the Attorney and/or Process Server server failed in his duty.

Service of process in cases filed in the United States district courts is governed by Rule 4 of the Federal Rules of Civil Procedure. Most state laws are based the Federal Rules. Each jurisdiction may also have rules regarding the means of service of process. Typically, a summons and related documents must be served upon the defendant personally, or in some cases upon another person of suitable age and discretion at the person's residence or place of business or employment. In some cases, service of process may be effected through the mail as in some small claims court procedures. In exceptional cases, other forms of service may be authorized by procedural rules or court order, including service by publication when an individual cannot be located in a particular jurisdiction.

Proper service of process initially establishes personal jurisdiction of the court over the person served. If the defendant ignores further pleadings or fails to participate in the proceedings, then the court or administrative body may find the defendant in default and award relief to the claimant, petitioner or plaintiff. Service of process must be distinguished from service of subsequent documents (such as pleadings and motion papers) between the parties to litigation.

Service on a defendant who resides in a country outside the jurisdiction of the Court must comply with special procedures prescribed under the *Hague Service Convention*[2], if the recipient's country is a signatory. Service on defendants in many South American countries and other countries is effected through the *Letter Rogatory process*[3].

Personal service

Personal service is service of process directly to the party named on the summons, complaint or petition. When serving a Corporation, LLC, LLP, or other business entity; personal service must be made to the "Registered Agent" of a business entity. A registered agent, also known as a resident agent or statutory agent, is a business or individual designated to receive service of process on behalf of the business entity. The registered agent for a business entity may be an individual member of the company, or (more often) a third party, such as the organization's lawyer or a service company.

Substituted service

When an individual party to be served is unavailable for personal service, many jurisdictions allow for substituted service. Substituted service allows the process server to leave service documents with another responsible individual such as cohabiting adults. Under the Federal Rules, substituted service may only be made at the abode or dwelling of the defendant. California, Illinois, and many other U.S. jurisdictions require that, in addition to substituted service, the documents be mailed to the

---

2 The Hague Service Convention, is a multilateral treaty which was signed in The Hague on 15 November 1965 by members of the Hague Conference on Private International Law. It allows service of judicial documents from one signatory state to another without recourse to consular and diplomatic channels.

3 A Letter Rogatory or Letter of Request is a formal request from a court to a foreign court for some type of judicial assistance. The most common remedies sought by Letters Rogatory are service of process and taking of evidence.

recipient. Substituted service often requires the serving party to show that ordinary service is impracticable and that substituted service will reach the party and effect notice. In addition, substituted service may be affected through public notice followed by sending the documents by Certified Mail.

Service by mail

Service by mail is permitted by most U.S. jurisdictions for service on defendants located in other U.S. states or foreign countries. Service by mail is not available if the country of destination has filed objections to service by mail pursuant to the multinational Hague Service Convention.

Service by publication

When a defendant's whereabouts are unknown, the Court may permit service by publication, usually in a newspaper. Service by publication is used to give "constructive notice" to a defendant who is intentionally absent, in hiding, unknown (as a possible descendant of a former landowner), and only when allowed by a judge's order based on a sworn declaration of the inability to find the defendant after due diligence. Service by publication is commonly used in a divorce action to serve a spouse who has disappeared without leaving a forwarding address or to give notice to people who might have a right to object to a "quiet title" action to clear title to real property.

Voluntary acceptance of service

As a substitute for personal service by a process server, many jurisdictions encourage voluntary acceptance of service, also called waiver of service (although other ways exist by which service of process may be waived). The summons and other documents are mailed to the party to be served, along with a request to sign and return a form of acceptance of service, or acknowledgment of service.

Acceptance of service means that the served party agrees to acknowledge receipt of the complaint or petition without the need to engage a process server. Failure to accept service voluntarily means that the party to be served will be liable for the cost of effecting formal service, even if the plaintiff's action is otherwise unsuccessful. In U.S. federal court, and in many state courts, voluntary acceptance of service entitles the defendant to more time to file an answer.

Serve or Post

Some processes are designated "Serve or Post"; of the most common are Landlord/Tenant orders (Evictions). These are most often served by the Sheriff or Constable in unregulated states but may also be served by Special Servers in regulated states. Rather than knock on a door and invite trouble, the server may post the document on the door or some apparent place on or nearby the dwelling.

If at all possible you should avoid using any sort of destructive method of attaching the document to the dwelling. A hammer and nails wont do; nor is duct-tape necessarily a good idea. It tends to grip too well and can cause damage to the surface finish or paint, resulting in liability for damages. Instead, there are a variety of quality removable all-weather tapes available from 3-M. While nothing is flawless, at least you can say you tried to be courteous. Just be sure that the documents stay put under high winds and rain. Of course you should try to avoid leaving the documents exposed to weather where a good rain may do enough damage to the documents to make a case for bad service. Wherever "Serve or Post" is concerned you must also mail a copy of the service via certified mail. You will then file two returns[4] with the court. One for the posted serve and an affidavit of Mailing.

---

[4] It is not uncommon for both the Affivavit and Sheriffs return to be casually called "returns" In this case "return" refers to any documents that must be filed after making service.

Sample: AFFIDAVIT OF MAILING

(Sample only. May not be legal in your jurisdiction)

I am over the age of eighteen years, and, on ___/___/___
I mailed a _____ (describe the paper or document mailed), a copy of which is attached, to the addressee set forth below, by depositing a copy enclosed in a postpaid wrapper, in an official depository under the exclusive care and custody of the United States Postal Service, in _____ (city, county, state), addressed as follows:

_____
(name and address of addressee).

Signature _____ Dated ___/___/___

------------------Notary------------------

SUBSCRIBED AND SWORN to before me this _____ day of _____, 20____, by _____

Proved to me on the basis of satisfactory evidence to be the person(s) who appeared before me.

SIGNATURE OF NOTARY PUBLIC.

_____

SEAL: _____ NOTARY PUBLIC

for the state of. _____

Affidavit of due diligence

An affidavit of due diligence attests that a process server has made reasonable effort in his attempt to serve process; or that the legal requirements thereof have been met. This affidavit is filed with the court in the event that the person to be served could not be located or otherwise cannot be served. The affidavit explains the efforts made by the process server, such as times and date of attempted service, investigations such as interviewing neighbors or skip trace. The purpose of the affidavit of due diligence is to show the court that all legal obligations have been met. The filing of a valid affidavit of due diligence may initiate or justify other methods of service, such as service by publication.

Sample: AFFIDAVIT OF DUE DILIGENCE WHERE SERVICE CANNOT BE PERFECTED

STATE OF _____ JURISDICTION OF: _____

In the interest of:
_____

Plaintiff ._____
vs.
Defendant/Respondent_____

Personally appeared before me, _____, the undersigned officer duly authorized to administer oaths, first being duly sworn, on oath deposes and states that he/she is not related to any party, has no interest in the above styled case, is not a convicted felon, is a resident of Colorado, and is a native born citizen of the United States of America.

Affiant further states that he/she attempted to serve the Defendant/Respondent through repeated attempts, however the defendant could not be served or would not provide an opportunity for service to be perfected despite the due diligence of the process server.

Service was attempted at the following locations on the dates and times given with the results as listed:

At: (This line will appear several times to demonstrate due diligence)
_____
Date: _____ Time: _____ Result: _____

Subscribed and sworn to before me in the county

of _____, State of Colorado,

this _____ day of _____, 2009.

Trespassing

In nearly every state of the United States, process servers are restricted from trespassing on property as a means of serving process. Such invasions, no matter how innocuous, are regarded as not only invalid, but illegal and may result in penalties for offenders. Gated communities and apartment buildings have created a difficulty for process servers, however, most are required to allow process servers to enter them.

In California, "Registered Process Servers" are granted "...a limited exemption against trespassing." This allows servers to enter a private property for a reasonable period of time to attempt service of process. Similarly, in California, gated communities which are "...staffed by a security guard, or where access is controlled, must allow a Registered Process Server to enter for service of process upon presenting valid identification, and indicating to which address the process server is going." This does not prevent the security guard from contacting the resident and alerting them that a process server is on his way to their residence. In Washington State, "Registered Process Servers" are granted a limited exemption or affirmative defense against trespassing. (see WA rules)

Deadlines

Most states have a deadline for completing service of process after filing of the summons and complaint. In New York, for example, service must be completed in 120 days after filing for almost all cases, and Hawaii State Circuit Court rule 28 requires service in a civil lawsuit must be effected within 6 months from commencing suit. In Pennsylvania the deadline is 30 days with the option of reissuing the order to effect an extension.

Dies non juridicum (Day without judiciary)

In some states and local jurisdictions, service of process may be prohibited be on Sundays, election days, certain holidays and on Saturdays where the party to be served counts Saturday as a day of religious observance. However, some states will allow the service of of process on dies non juridicum under special circumstances; such as when service of process is pursuant to a court order.

Chapter IV

Federal Rules of Civil Procedure (2006)
(incorporating the revisions which took effect Dec. 1, 2006)

The following is taken from the Federal Rules of Civil Procedure The rules of each state are based largely on the Federal model. It is critical that you become familiar with Federal rules, and then your own states rules, before engaging in the service of process.

II. COMMENCEMENT OF ACTION; SERVICE OF PROCESS, PLEADINGS, MOTIONS, AND ORDERS

Rule 1. - Scope and Purpose of Rules

These rules govern the procedure in the United States district courts in all suits of a civil nature whether cognizable as cases at law or in equity or in admiralty, with the exceptions stated in Rule 81. They shall be construed and administered to secure the just, speedy, and inexpensive determination of every action.

Rule 2. One Form of Action

There shall be one form of action to be known as "civil action."

Rule 3. Commencement of Action

A civil action is commenced by filing a complaint with the court.

Rule 4. Summons

The summons shall be signed by the clerk, bear the seal of the court, identify the court and the parties, be directed to the defendant, and state the name and address of the plaintiff's attorney or, if unrepresented, of the plaintiff. It shall also state the time within which the defendant must appear and defend, and notify the defendant that failure to do so will result in a judgment by default against the defendant for the relief demanded in the complaint. The court may allow a summons to be amended.

(b) Issuance.

Upon or after filing the complaint, the plaintiff may present a summons to the clerk for signature and seal. If the summons is in proper form, the clerk shall sign, seal, and issue it to the plaintiff for service on the defendant. A summons, or a copy of the summons if addressed to multiple defendants, shall be issued for each defendant to be served.

(c) Service with Complaint; by Whom Made.

(1) A summons shall be served together with a copy of the complaint. The plaintiff is responsible for service of a summons and complaint within the time allowed under subdivision (m) and

shall furnish the person effecting service with the necessary copies of the summons and complaint.

(2) Service may be effected by any person who is not a party and who is at least 18 years of age. At the request of the plaintiff, however, the court may direct that service be effected by a United States marshal, deputy United States marshal, or other person or officer specially appointed by the court for that purpose. Such an appointment must be made when the plaintiff is authorized to proceed in forma pauperis pursuant to 28 U.S.C. § 1915 or is authorized to proceed as a seaman under 28 U.S.C. § 1916.

(d) Waiver of Service; Duty to Save Costs of Service; Request to Waive.

(1) A defendant who waives service of a summons does not thereby waive any objection to the venue or to the jurisdiction of the court over the person of the defendant.

(2) An individual, corporation, or association that is subject to service under subdivision (e), (f), or (h) and that receives notice of an action in the manner provided in this paragraph has a duty to avoid unnecessary costs of serving the summons. To avoid costs, the plaintiff may notify such a defendant of the commencement of the action and request that the defendant waive service of a summons. The notice and request

(A) shall be in writing and shall be addressed directly to the defendant, if an individual, or else to an officer or managing or general agent (or other agent authorized by appointment or law to receive service of process) of a defendant subject to service under subdivision (h);

(B) shall be dispatched through first-class mail or other reliable means;

(C) shall be accompanied by a copy of the complaint and shall identify the court in which it has been filed;

(D) shall inform the defendant, by means of a text prescribed in an official form promulgated pursuant to Rule 84, of the consequences of compliance and of a failure to comply with the request;

(E) shall set forth the date on which request is sent;

(F) shall allow the defendant a reasonable time to return the waiver, which shall be at least 30 days from the date on which the request is sent, or 60 days from that date if the defendant is addressed outside any judicial district of the United States; and

(G) shall provide the defendant with an extra copy of the notice and request, as well as a prepaid means of compliance in writing.

If a defendant located within the United States fails to comply with a request for waiver made by a plaintiff located within the United States, the court shall impose the costs subsequently incurred in effecting service on the defendant unless good cause for the failure be shown.

(3) A defendant that, before being served with process, timely returns a waiver so requested is not required to serve an answer to the complaint until 60 days after the date on which the request for waiver of service was sent, or 90 days after that date if the defendant was addressed outside any judicial district of the United States.

(4) When the plaintiff files a waiver of service with the court, the action shall proceed, except as provided in paragraph (3), as if a summons and complaint had been served at the time of filing the waiver, and no proof of service shall be required.

(5) The costs to be imposed on a defendant under paragraph (2) for failure to comply with a request to waive service of a summons shall include the costs subsequently incurred in effecting service under subdivision (e), (f), or (h), together with the costs, including a reasonable attorney's fee, of any motion required to collect the costs of service.

(e) Service Upon Individuals Within a Judicial District of the United States.

Unless otherwise provided by federal law, service upon an individual from whom a waiver has not been obtained and filed, other than an infant or an incompetent person, may be effected in any judicial district of the United States:

(1) pursuant to the law of the state in which the district court is located, or in which service is effected, for the service of a summons upon the defendant in an action brought in the courts of general jurisdiction of the State; or

(2) by delivering a copy of the summons and of the complaint to the individual personally or by leaving copies thereof at the individual's dwelling house or usual place of abode with some person of suitable age and discretion then residing therein or by delivering a copy of the summons and of the complaint to an agent authorized by appointment or by law to receive service of process.

(f) Service Upon Individuals in a Foreign Country.

Unless otherwise provided by federal law, service upon an individual from whom a waiver has not been obtained and filed, other than an infant or an incompetent person, may be effected in a place not within any judicial district of the United States:

(1) by any internationally agreed means reasonably calculated to give notice, such as those means authorized by the Hague Convention on the Service Abroad of Judicial and Extrajudicial Documents; or

(2) if there is no internationally agreed means of service or the applicable international agreement allows other means of service, provided that service is reasonably calculated to give notice:

(A) in the manner prescribed by the law of the foreign country for service in that country in an action in any of its courts of general jurisdiction; or

(B) as directed by the foreign authority in response to a letter rogatory or letter of request; or

(C) unless prohibited by the law of the foreign country, by

(i) delivery to the individual personally of a copy of the summons and the complaint; or

(ii) any form of mail requiring a signed receipt, to be addressed and dispatched by the clerk of the court to the party to be served; or

(3) by other means not prohibited by international agreement as may be directed by the court.

(g) Service Upon Infants and Incompetent Person.

Service upon an infant or an incompetent person in a judicial district of the United States shall be effected in the manner prescribed by the law of the state in which the service is made for the service of summons or like process upon any such defendant in an action brought in the courts of general jurisdiction of that state. Service upon an infant or an incompetent person in a place not within any judicial district of the United States shall be effected in the manner prescribed by paragraph (2)(A) or (2)(B) of subdivision (f) or by such means as the court may direct.

(h) Service Upon Corporations and Associations.

Unless otherwise provided by federal law, service upon a domestic or foreign corporation or upon a partnership or other unincorporated association that is subject to suit under a common name, and from which a waiver of service has not been obtained and filed, shall be effected:

(1) in a judicial district of the United States in the manner prescribed for individuals by subdivision (e)(1), or by delivering a copy of the summons and of the complaint to an officer, a managing or general agent, or to any other agent authorized by appointment or by law to receive service of process and, if the agent is one authorized by statute to receive service and the statute so requires, by also mailing a copy to the defendant, or

(2) in a place not within any judicial district of the United States in any manner prescribed for individuals by subdivision (f) except personal delivery as provided in paragraph (2)(C)(i) thereof.

(i) Serving the United States, Its Agencies, Corporations, Officers, or Employees.

(1) Service upon the United States shall be effected

(A) by delivering a copy of the summons and of the complaint to the United States attorney for the district in which the action is brought or to an assistant United States attorney or clerical employee designated by the United States attorney in a writing filed with the clerk of the court or by sending a copy of the summons and of the complaint by registered or certified mail addressed to the civil process clerk at the office of the United States attorney and

(B) by also sending a copy of the summons and of the complaint by registered or certified mail to the Attorney General of the United States at Washington, District of Columbia, and

(C) in any action attacking the validity of an order of an officer or agency of the United States not made a party, by also sending a copy of the summons and of the complaint by registered or certified mail to the officer or agency.

(2)

(A) Service on an agency or corporation of the United States, or an officer or employee of the United States sued only in an official capacity, is effected by serving the United States in the manner prescribed by Rule 4(i)(1) and by also sending a copy of the summons and complaint by registered or certified mail to the officer, employee, agency, or corporation.

(B)Service on an officer or employee of the United States sued in an individual capacity for acts or omissions occurring in connection with the performance of duties on behalf of the United States - whether or not the officer or employee is sued also in an official capacity - is effected by serving the United States in the manner prescribed by Rule 4(i)(1) and by serving the officer or employee in the manner prescribed by Rule 4 (e), (f), or (g).

(3) The court shall allow a reasonable time to serve process under Rule 4(i) for the purpose of curing the failure to serve:

(A) all persons required to be served in an action governed by Rule 4(i)(2)(A), if the plaintiff has served either the United States attorney or the Attorney General of the United States, or

(B) the United States in an action governed by Rule 4(i)(2)(B), if the plaintiff has served an officer or employee of the United States sued in an individual capacity.

(j) Service Upon Foreign, State, or Local Governments.

(1) Service upon a foreign state or a political subdivision, agency, or instrumentality thereof shall be effected pursuant to 28 U.S.C. § 1608.

(2) Service upon a state, municipal corporation, or other governmental organization subject to suit, shall be effected by delivering a copy of the summons and of the complaint to its chief executive officer or by serving the summons and complaint in the manner prescribed by the law of that state for the service of summons or other like process upon any such defendant.

(k) Territorial Limits of Effective Service.

(1) Service of a summons or filing a waiver of service is effective to establish jurisdiction over the person of a defendant

(A) who could be subjected to the jurisdiction of a court of general jurisdiction in the state in which the district court is located, or

(B) who is a party joined under Rule 14 or Rule 19 and is served at a place within a judicial district of the United States and not more than 100 miles from the place from which the summons issues, or

(C) who is subject to the federal interpleader jurisdiction under 28 U.S.C. § 1335, or

(D) when authorized by a statute of the United States.

(2) If the exercise of jurisdiction is consistent with the Constitution and laws of the United States, serving a summons or filing a waiver of service is also effective, with respect to claims arising under federal law, to establish personal jurisdiction over the person of any defendant who is not subject to the jurisdiction of the courts of general jurisdiction of any state.

(l) Proof of Service.

If service is not waived, the person effecting service shall make proof thereof to the court. If service is made by a person other than a United States marshal or deputy United States marshal, the person shall make affidavit thereof. Proof of service in a place not within any judicial district of the United States shall, if effected under paragraph (1) of subdivision (f), be made pursuant to the applicable treaty or convention, and shall, if effected under paragraph (2) or (3) thereof, include a receipt signed by the addressee or other evidence of delivery to the addressee satisfactory to the court. Failure to make proof of service does not affect the validity of the service. The court may allow proof of service to be amended.

(m) Time Limit for Service.

If service of the summons and complaint is not made upon a defendant within 120 days after the filing of the complaint, the court, upon motion or on its own initiative after notice to the plaintiff, shall dismiss the action without prejudice as to that defendant or direct that service be effected within a specified time; provided that if the plaintiff shows good cause for the failure, the court shall extend the time for service for an appropriate period. This subdivision does not apply to service in a foreign country pursuant to subdivision (f) or (j)(1).

(n) Seizure of Property; Service of Summons not Feasible.

(1) If a statute of the United States so provides, the court may assert jurisdiction over property. Notice to claimants of the property shall than be sent in the manner provided by the statute or by service of a summons under this rule.

(2) Upon a showing that personal jurisdiction over a defendant cannot, in the district where the action is brought, be obtained with reasonable efforts by service of summons in any manner authorized by this rule, the court may assert jurisdiction over any of the defendant's assets found within the district by seizing the assets under the circumstances and in the manner provided by the law of the state in which the district court is located.

Test your knowledge

Answer True or False.

1. Federal rules of service always overrule state rules.

2. In cases of service-out-of-state, process must be served according to the rules of the state in which service will be made.

3. Only licensed and registered Process Servers are considered officers of the court.

4. Process servers in unregulated states are not required to be insured or bonded.

5. An Agent of the court is the same as an Officer.

6. In most cases, a summons may be served via substituted service at ones primary place of employment.

7. Process Servers have the universal right to trespass in the service of ones duty.

8. It is illegal in all states to serve process on Sundays and national holidays.

9. Subpoenas drawn-up by individual attorneys require that process server be especially appointed by that attorney.

10. Failure to file proof of service invalidates the service.

Chapter V
Serving Process

State Rules

While the rules of each state are similar to the federal rules, each state has unique laws that you, as a process server, need to know and understand. In fact, you need to carefully review the rules of every state for which you handle service. In general, when handling out-of-state paper, the rules of the state in which the summons or subpoena originated determine the rules of service; even though service will ultimately be executed in your state. Therefore, you should first comprehend the federal rules, then those of your state. Then, always double-check the state rules from which out-of-state paper originates. Rules change. In addition, some cities have their own rules for service, which may differ from the rest of the state.

You can easily obtain a copy of each state's rules on their respective web sites and you should always go directly to the source. Try to avoid taking information from third party sites offering civil rules for each state. Many process service agencies publish these rules but they rarely update them.

Modes of Personal Service

Personal service is not restricted to hand-to-hand transfer of documents. In fact, personal service may be valid even if the served party refuses to accept the documents or even refuses to acknowledge your presence. In this section we will explore the various modes of personal service.

Hand-to-hand Service

The most desirable and least contested form of personal service is hand-to-hand Service. In this mode of personal service you, the server, are in the presence of the person to be served, have established their identity and have personally hand them the documents to be served. Once they take the documents from you it does not matter whether they tear them up, throw then to the ground or roll them up and smoke them. What matters is that you made personal service. However, if you witness such behavior you should take note of it in your journal in case you are called to testify on your own behalf.

Service by touch

A secondary mode of personal service is service by touch. In this mode of service the person to be served may be reluctant to receive the documents or they may ignore you and attempt to walk or run away. In order to make service by touch the scenario must meet all of the same qualifications as hand-to-hand service except that it is not necessary for the person being served to physically take the documents from you. Once you have positively established their identity you may execute service by verbally informing the individual that they are being served with legal process and then physically touching them with the documents. Once that is established you may allow the documents to fall to the ground. It does not matter whether the individual picks them up, service has been made. This form of service requires that you have clearly communicated the service of process to the individual and that you can make physical contact with them by touching them with the documents. (Not with your bare hands) Your return will indicate personal service by touch and should succinctly explain the exact situation that transpired requiring service by touch.

Service by Refusal

Another form of personal service is service by refusal. Similar to service by touch, this mode of service usually requires that the individual has confirmed his or her identity, but refuses to accept service. Otherwise you must have strong evidence that this is indeed the person you think it is. If the scenario meets all the requirements of service by touch except that you are unable to make physical contact with the individual, you may verbally inform them that they are being served process and you may leave the documents on a doorstep or desk, or even on the ground. It is important, however, that there is an expectation that the documents will be retrievable after you leave the scene. Therefore, dropping the documents on a train platform, as the train pulls away, would not be an ideal place to leave the papers. If it is reasonable to expect that the documents are not retrievable, it was probably not good service. Service by refusal should demonstrate that the person being served knew they were being served and that they knowingly refused to accept or retrieve the documents through no fault of action of your own.

Ultimately, whether or not you have made good service is based on a matter of your word as the process server, which should stand up to scrutiny if called into question. You may be required to testify on your own behalf.

Verbal Service

Verbal service is the most tenuous form of personal service because it is usually only necessary when the person being served has refused to acknowledge their identity and also refuses to acknowledge you. In short, they are ignoring you. In this case, as long as you can remain in their physical presence, you may read process to them verbally. There are few imaginable situations in which this scenario would develop but is does happen from time to time. Process servers have been known to chase along as a person to be served rushes through a lengthy airport terminal to catch a plane. With verbal service you must know for sure, somehow, that you are speaking to the right person (their intent silence is usually confirmation) and you must also know for sure that they can hear you. They must remain in your presence throughout the recitation. If they board a plane before you finish your song you may not be able to say for sure that they heard you. To play it safe, you must know for sure. The advent of Blutetooth headsets and earphones has added a degree of uncertainty to verbal service; and a potential defense.

Service by Phone

It happens. At some point you will be asked to serve a subpoena to a known bad address but with a valid phone or mobile number. In this case all your sleuthing techniques go right out the window. You have but one option; make the call and be straightforward. Just as in person, you need to first confirm the identity of the individual and then you may execute Verbal Service by phone. Sure, they may hang up on you mid-sentence; but that's assuming that they don't want to be served. As previously mentioned, most people are unaware they are going to be served and will at least hear your out. Others may be elated, or devastated, by the news of their divorce proceedings.

If, once you have established your intention, they don't want to be served, they COULD hang up, but chances are they will be curious enough to hear you out. Just as in verbal personal service you must know for sure that they did indeed hear you and your return should reflect any such evidence. Of course, impersonal verbal service is a last resort and subject to the rules of the appropriate jurisdiction.

Service on minors and incompetents

You may be called to execute service on a minor or a person who is legally incompetent; for example, a person suffering from dementia or who is mentally disabled. In this case it is best to make arrangements for a competent witness to be present as you read the service aloud to both the individual to be served and their witness. You may then leave the documents with the witness. Acceptable witnesses include parents, children of adequate age to be served, legal guardians and individuals with power of attorney. Often these may include personal nurses, designated representatives at hospital facilities and elderly care communities. In any event the issuing attorney should direct you with advice in the matter and, if it turns out that he was unaware of the situation, you should contact him with this information before attempting service. It could be critical to his case.

Making Service

When you receive a fresh batch of documents from the issuing attorney or clerk you should carefully look over each to check for inaccuracies or omissions which could impede your ability to make timely service. Ask whether or not the address provided is believed to be valid. Also compare the address on all the forms to be certain that they all match. One missing or incorrect digit can make the difference between a quick-paying serve and a long drawn-out case at your expense.

It would be nice if every attempt to serve was simple and straightforward. You would knock on the door of every residence to find the person you are looking for will cordially accept service. Unfortunately, reality dictates otherwise. No two serves are exactly the same and some are, well, less than simple. Fortunately, most serves are of the "typical" sort. Most people are not aware they are going to be served and are generally taken by surprise. In the best example of a simple serve, you will have relatively easy access to the individual. It is usually a matter of knocking on a door and waiting for an answer. With luck, the person you are seeking will answer the door in which case it is a simple matter of establishing their identity and executing service.

When making service at a residence, if the person standing in front of you COULD be your target, (not a Woman when you are looking for a Man) it is best to assume that they are the person you are looking for. Rather than asking them who they are, simply say "Mr. Smith, I have some urgent legal documents for you." But do not hand them the documents yet! Wait for confirmation of identity. If they are not Mr. Smith they will waste no time telling you. In which case you will say. "I'm sorry, I have to deliver these documents to Mr. Smith". This will provide an opportunity to determine if substituted service can be made on the individual in front of you. (If they are a spouse or resident family-member) If not, you may be able to obtain useful information as to where you may find Mr. Smith. Of course, you must have confirmation of their identity either way before handing over the documents.

If you are able to make service by handing the forms to Mr. Smith try to avoid saying the words "you have been served". This will probably be perceived as rude and could draw you into a conflict. Instead, simply hand over the papers and explain, briefly that all the details are enclosed. Then leave promptly.

Sometimes you will encounter an individual at the given address who will inform you that the person you are seeking no longer lives there. This may or may not be true. Perhaps they have moved away; taken a vacation; been incarcerated; have gone into hiding; or died. Or, perhaps, they do indeed live there. Never take at face value what you are told by another resident. They may or not be telling the truth, but it is ultimately your responsibility to verify any information which they may provide.

The first step is to simply determine if the current resident has any useful information to share. They may or may not; but this will give you the opportunity to judge their character. If they seem sincere you may decide to proceed based on what information you have been given. Even if they offer nothing, that is still something! If you are fairly certain that the resident really has no idea who you are seeking, you will probably not waste time staking out that residence. On the contrary, if you are sure they are lying you may be prompted to do a little snooping; which may involve interviewing neighbors or staking out the property.

When dealing with apartment complexes a new resident is unlikely to know anything about the past resident. If the current resident says they have only lived there for a few weeks or months, this may indicate that the person you are seeking has indeed relocated. In addition, in todays economy, it is not uncommon to arrive at an address to find it has been foreclosed upon. In such a case it may be advantageous to check with neighbors for more information.

Once you have determined that the subject no longer resides at the address given, you have a few options. First, ask the attorney who hired you to either interview his client or have them contact you to obtain additional information about the person to served. In most cases they know one another.

Another easy lead is the local post office where you can check for a change of address. You can also try calling the last known phone number to see if a new phone number has been assigned. If so, cross check that with the phone book for an address. Since phone books are only issued annually you may try the Internet version of the phone book which is updated more frequently. Of course, there is still the old method of calling directory assistance.

The advent of social network web-communities has proven a boon for finding people who can otherwise not be found. It is amazing what people will post for all the world to see, even when they have gone to great lengths to cover their real-world tracks. See if the plaintiff knows the on line identities of the person being sought. Otherwise you can start searching the Internet using their legal name or aliases. Beyond this, you get into the area of skip-tracing.

Skip-tracing is the art and science of locating an individual who does not want to be found. In essence, they have "skipped out". Skip-tracing follows the paper-trail they leave in everyday life. In other words, detective work. In most jurisdictions it is entirely acceptable for you to apply skip-trace methods in the duty of service of process. Otherwise, it would be entirely illegal for you to do so without a private investigator license.

Skip-trace methods include research of credit reporting services, drivers records, public records and more. Skip-tracing is a learned discipline that is beyond the scope of this book. There are a variety of books and resources that cover this topic in detail. I recommend starting with the *Complete Idiots Guide to Private Investigating*; Second Edition, by Steven Kerry Brown

Difficult Individuals

It is not uncommon, particularly when making service at a residence, that the person you are looking to serve will be evasive or even lie right to your face. Relatives are naturally protective and are reluctant to divulge much information to a stranger.

In many cases a professional appearance, attitude and direct language will help bridge the gap. It is always acceptable to explain that you are legal process server and that you are charged by the court to deliver time sensitive court documents. In most cases saying less accomplishes more. Sputtering out too much information only gives the person at the door an opportunity to say nothing. State your intension and then listen. Straight eye contact and a moment or two of awkward silence can go a long way. Even if you don't get the information you want, with practice, observing peoples' behavior will often reveal useful information. Rule 1. Don't fear the silence! Rule 2. Listen Listen Listen.

Sometimes when making service on a female, a husband or boyfriend may attempt to "manage" you. But if you find yourself in a situation where this becomes a problem you have already overstayed your welcome. Remember, you can execute personal service as long as the served party is visibly and audibly present. If ever there is a situation where it is OK to say "you have been served" this may be it.

Very often the person at the door will tell you that they are not who you are looking for. These situations take finesse and each is different. If you are certain that the person before you is the person you are looking for you could say "I believe you are Mr. Smith and you have been served legal process"

Of course, you must have good reason to assume this is the person you were supposed to serve. Sometimes a description of the party will be provided with the documents, or you may contact the attorney who issued the subpoena and ask him to obtain a description from the plaintiff.

Perhaps you have made three attempts at service and the same person answers the door every time, but he refuses to acknowledge his true identity. If your surveillance indicates that he is the only person living in the house, and he matches a description, you may feel confident of his identity. But Never Guess. Due diligence is the rule.[5]

One server had been turned away at the door several times by the same person. From surveillance, he knew that the individual left is home every day at around 4:00 and walked to a convenience store on the corner. One day the server followed him. Just before the individual entered the store he had to pass through a group of loiters outside. At this point the server shouted "Mike!" causing the individual (Michael Smith) to respond. When Mike turned around the server tapped him on the sleeve with the documents and said" This is subpoena for you" and let the papers fall to the ground. Note that the crowd of

---

[5] Some servers will snap a discreet picture of the individual using a mobile phone or hidden camera. This could seal your case should the person in the picture claim that he was not served; but this practice can be dangerous because it often sparks hostility. Use discretion.

people helped establish that only Mike would respond. Had they been alone it is reasonable that anyone would have at least turned around if someone was shouting behind him.

Sometimes people are constructively evasive. In one instance a server attempted to make service at the home of a man who had a gated entrance to a long drive leading up to his house. The process server simply could not gain access to the man without trespassing. He tried waiting at the gate for the man to arrive home but the man just drove past him and the gate swung shut behind him. The individual simply did not want to be served.

So, in wait for the man to arrive home one afternoon, the server parked his car on the shoulder of the road in front of the pull-off to the gate. He turned on his vehicle hazard lights and popped open the hood. There he waited, fiddling with the engine so as to appear that his car had broken down. When the man arrived home he beeped a few times, shouted a few obscenities and, eventually, got out of the car to "help" push the disabled vehicle away from his drive. When he did so, the server dropped the hood, touched the man with the documents and said, "it was just a loose cable, and this is a subpoena."

This is a potentially dangerous method that is not endorsed or recommended, but it does demonstrate how Special servers sometimes need to be creative within the confines of the law.

Dealing with the gatekeeper

Recall the scenario where we were attempting to execute service on Mr. Spencer. Presently, we are still in the lobby patiently awaiting his audience

By this time it has become clear that the receptionist has no intention of allowing you to see Mr. Spencer. The next offensive would be to make your legal case. Both Federal and State rules of process have stipulations concerning the obstruction of the service of process. In most states it is at least a misdemeanor to impede the service of process. At this point you may want to read your state rules concerning obstruction of a process server aloud in a firm and boisterous voice, for all those in the lobby to hear. This should make your point clear. If not, you may offer top call the police to report the misdemeanor. The police may or may not respond, but if they do, you should be prepared to explain the conditions under which you called them and the law regarding obstruction of service. Never threaten to call the police if you really have no intention of doing so. You may, however, ask the receptionist if it will be necessary to do so. You may want to carry your state rules concerning obstruction of service on a wallet-card just for these situations. Later we will discuss the use of a rules card in tandem with proper identification.

Exercise: Review your state rules and identify the specific rule pertaining to the obstruction of service of process and the legal ramifications thereof.

Interviewing Neighbors

Occasionally it will be necessary to ask around the neighborhood for information about the person to be served. Some neighbors may be protective of their friends and refuse to offer any helpful advice. Others may be indifferent or even hostile toward the person to be served; and therefore more willing to help. In any case, the process server should exercise utmost discretion. Inquiries should be limited to establishing that an individual resides at the dwelling in question; the known whereabouts of an individual; or when they tend to arrive home from work. If you feel it necessary to explain why you are looking for an individual it will suffice to explain that you have some important legal documents to deliver to them. Generally, if a neighbor is disinterested in offering this information is it not worth pursuing any further. In rare instances it may be necessary to produce some identification to establish your intention. It is entirely acceptable to do so if it provides a hesitant neighbor piece of mind that you are not a hired assassin; but identification should NEVER be used to coerce a non-party to offer any cooperation, particularly where *Badges* are concerned.

Attitude and Demeanor

In every case, it is important to be direct, but professional, in order to execute a safe and effective service. The demeanor of the process server should be cordial yet authoritative. You should never seem apologetic or uncertain of your duty. Try not to end any sentence with a question mark. Instead of saying "Are you mister Smith". You will say, "'Mr. Smith, I have legal documents for you". Never allow yourself to be drawn into an explanation and never give advice as to what the person being served should do. Simply explain that the details are on the papers and thank them. Wishing them a "good day" is probably not appropriate because you probably just ruined their day. Use common sense.

Keeping a Journal

From the very first day you begin to work as a process server you should begin keeping a written journal of each service. A busy server can make several serves per day and you will quickly begin to forget details related to each and every case. It is therefore essential that you keep a journal of your experiences. Some servers prefer to take field notes using a voice recorder and than transcribe those notes to text back at the office. It is important to keep good notes that are readily retrievable in case you are ever called to testify.

Your journal should contain the following information:

- Day, Date and Time of service.
- Details about the person to be served including the same information that appears at the top of the subpoena or summons; name and address of individual(s) to be served and the attorney/court issuing the subpoena. Any notes or advice given to you by the issuing attorney should also be included; such as a description of the individual you are seeking.
- Any difficulties encountered during the serve: Extra hours spent doing surveillance or investigation, (for billing purposes and to demonstrate due diligence) and of course the details any surveillance and investigation.
- Who accepted the documents; Names and description.
- The mode of service: Hand-to-hand, touch, refusal etc.
- Any additional details that could be important to future testimony concerning the service.

Due Diligence

Every process server is expected to exercise due diligence in the performance of his duty. But what is due diligence? The amount of time and resources expended by the server will depend on a variety of factors; not the least of which are those established by their employer. The larger Process Service clearinghouses often only expect their employees or contractors to make one or two attempts before giving up and returning to home base. Often they will simply issue you a new assignment and pass your unserved documents to the next in line to make service. Perhaps a specialist, perhaps an official, or perhaps they will file non-est and that will be that.

When working for yourself, such a severe lack of due diligence would be your undoing. Every serve you make is money in the bank. Every serve you fail is time and money wasted. In addition, every time you file a return of non-est you do a little damage to your reputation. A server who consistently fails to make service can expect the phone to ring considerably less in the near future.

It is not unusual to make two to three attempts before finding an individual at home or at their place of employment. The trick is to make your efforts efficient. You should be working on several cases at a time. You can check back on harder serves as you travel throughout your day or week. If you have the time to focus exclusively on one case, you are under worked; unless you are being paid by the hour for surveillance and investigation.

If you are dealing with a known evasive subject or a questionable address, you should be charging by the hour. A typical hourly rate for a hard serve involving research and surveillance can range from $20 to $60.00 per hour. To determine the going rates in your area contact a licensed private investigator to inquire for their hourly field surveillance fee. Then aim slightly below that.

In summary, your Non-Est return and affidavit of due diligence needs to show that you make a reasonable effort to effect service on every case. Remember, if you don't make service, someone else will get paid for it.

So, what constitutes due diligence? At least three descent attempts.

Uniform, Dress, Supplies

A good process server wears allot of hats, and coats, and other sundry items for a variety of reasons. Every server needs a good suit. You will wear this when visiting Law offices and when making service at businesses and public places. In fact, anywhere you can wear a suit, you should. In addition, you may need a good pair of boots, a flashlight, a local map (perhaps also GPS) and rain gear.

In your vehicle, you should also carry a set of clothes that will allow you to blend in while visiting neighborhoods where a suit or uniform could make you a target for crime.

Some process-service companies have their servers wear some sort of delivery/utility uniform or a business casual uniform consisting of slacks and a logo golf-shirt.

When it comes to dress there are some things you can not wear. As a general rule you can not misrepresent yourself. This means you should never pose as someone you are not by wearing the logo of a delivery company, utility, or anything that is a deliberate misrepresentation of your intention; particularly law-enforcement or the US postal service. You are also not allowed to fool people into accepting service by posing as a pizza delivery person. These kinds of disguises are deliberately deceptive and could cost the attorney his case and you your reputation. Most attorneys don't like their servers playing games; although, some would reward it.

That said, many servers wear generic work-gear that somewhat resembles typical delivery or service uniforms. This provides them with some degree of credibility in less than desirable neighborhoods and it is covert without being deceptive. Some servers even keep their documents inside a cardboard box that may or may not look like a package. This, however, is bordering on misrepresentation. Carrying the documents on a clip-board or clip-box would be just fine. In fact, the metal box-type clipboards are great for readying your serve and then taking notes for your journal as you exit the scene.

If you choose to use such a uniform, or disguise, remember never to use a corporate logo that does not belong to you and never pretend to be doing someone else's job.

Badges and ID

The issue of whether a Process Server needs to carry a Badge or *Shield* is controversial. While some regulated states issue photo Id's to licensed process servers, there is no US jurisdiction in which Process Servers are issued shields. The practice presumably stems from the fact that licensed Private Investigators, in some states, are issued Shields from the government and their licensed status gives them some advantage when conducting investigations. As such, Process Servers have begun to self-issue shields in the belief that the appearance of authority can make their job easier under certain circumstances. This practice is risky, but somewhat true. First, it must be stated that no process server Needs to carry a shield. Certainly the vast majority of servers do not have them; but on the other hand, the majority work for large firms that deal in high volumes of paper but exercise less diligence in making service. The question is; Under what circumstance would a process server need to possess and/or use a shield?

Many Process Servers report that using a shield, in tandem with their paper identification; can ease tensions during a complicated serve. In one such case, a process server was making service upon an elderly woman in a very bad neighborhood. He knocked on the door of her residence as she peered through a small, thick reinforced glass window. The door and glass were so secure that it was difficult to hear the woman as she shouted that she would call the police if the server did not go away. It was obvious that the old woman just did not know what the server wanted and she probably had a policy of never opening the door for someone she did not know. Since communication through the door was difficult, the server held up his Shield and ID to the window and gestured that he meant no harm. The woman became calm and opened the door a crack. The server explained to the woman that he was not a police officer but a process server who needed to deliver court papers to her. He then asked if she understood all this and she said "yes". Of course, his return probably omitted the specific mention of a badge. "Showed ID" would suffice.

This is a case where limited use of a shield was used to project the appearance of authority in a positive way.

Many servers who once scoffed at the idea of wearing a shield have changed their minds when they have seen its usefulness at locations where they frequently encounter a front-desk; such as business centers, hospitals and anywhere that security stands between the server and his target.

People who regularly deal with the public, like security and receptionists, don't tend to remember too many faces unless they see them regularly. But, they will remember a shield and this will help them remember YOU. Many servers report being waved past security or reception in places where they make frequent service because their shield reminds the person at the desk who they are and why they are here. Rather than go through the whole explanation on every visit, they may enjoy freedom of movement. But such a relationship is built on trust. No one should use a shield as a weapon and simply try to barge past reception or security on the first visit. When openly wearing a shield you should first approach reception as you normally would, explain your presence and intention and then, over time, you will be recognized and allowed to go about your business unimpeded.

Let's return to our first scenario where the receptionist has refused to allow you to see Mr. Spencer. At this point you have identified yourself, explained your intent and authority, probably more than once, and have recited your states rules regarding the obstruction of service. Having those rules on paper is helpful in this situation because some servers will make it a point to allow their shield to flash while they reach into the badge-wallet to produce the written rule card. This reinforces authority while not making any particular statement. Some servers would go so far as to present their badge and ID along with the written rules to establish that those rules apply to the current situation. This appearance of authority may be just enough to instill the legitimacy and seriousness of the situation.

NOTE: The use of Badges by non-law-enforcement for any reason is ILLEGAL in some states and local jurisdictions. In such states process servers should NEVER carry a badge on-the-job. Exactly which states and jurisdictions have restrictions on the use of Badges is beyond the scope of this book. You are encouraged to contact your local Sheriff to inquire about any such restrictions. Make sure they provide you with the statute or rule which restricts badge use. It is not uncommon for law-enforcement to indicate the use of badges is illegal, even when it is not. In most cases, they just don't know.

Shield Styles

There are a variety of ready-made Process Server badges available on the Internet and in law enforcement catalogs. They are usually inscribed with something like "Authorized Process Server" and bear a US federal seal. These are garbage. Never use one of these shields!

A Badge/Shield is a form of ID. The best practice for self-issuing badges is to formally incorporate your business (more on that later) and then have the company itself issue the badge. Further, the company name should be inscribed on the badge. This is where the generic "Authorized Process Server" badges fall short. Who is doing the authorizing? The center seal used on those generic badges indicates the Federal Government. Unless you are serving process for the US Supreme Court, you are not being "Authorized" by the Federal Government. That in itself is misrepresentation. Instead, your badge should indicate that you are an AGENT of your company. This legitimizes the badge as a company ID (as long as you legally incorporate your company) A good badge design would state something like:

SPECIAL
KEYSTONE PROCEDURAL
(Seal)

AUTHORIZED AGENT

PROCESS SERVER

(The center seal is a standard Scales of Justice logo)

Different types of Badges or Shields are associated with various types of authority. It is best not to choose a shield that resembles those of your local law enforcement or which are generally identifiable with a specific kind of public service office. For example, everyone recognizes the old-west style 5 point star as the Sheriff or Marshal.

Stars with 5-6 points: Marshal or Sheriffs Department

Stars with 7-8 points: Law Enforcement, Public Safety, Search & Rescue in some areas.

Knights-Shield-style: Police Patrol. Security, Detective.

Oval: Police / Detectives.

Maltese Cross: Exclusively Fire Department.

Eagle-crest over shield or circle: Emergency Medial Services.

This leaves the specialty-style badges such as circles, squares and other variations for other types of authorities. Unfortunately, it is becoming increasingly common for traditional law enforcement agencies to choose these ornate styles for their departments. Because these styles do not traditionally belong to one particular branch of service, there is no reason not to use them unless your local authorities already use them.

Some shield styles are specifically designed for "officers of the court". Although the selection is limited these types of shield tend to have elements of style that are associated with the legal system such as laurels, scales and architectural columns. These are perfect for process service agencies.

When purchasing a badge you should consider how you intend to use it. It is bad form to pin a badge to your shirt or sling it from your belt. Invest in a custom fitted leather bill-fold style case. These can be hung from a chain around the neck to display or conceal the shield. They also have a clear panel to display your company ID or state license. If you carry it in your breast pocket like a wallet it can be conveniently flipped open to flash the shield when you draw on your written rules card.

A quality badge in a quality case makes a statement of legitimacy. A cheap pre-fabricated badge dangling from your pocket button hole screams "Cop-wannabee".

Note that some states restrict the use of their state seals for government officials only. Also, in regulated States the use of a badge may be restricted. In other words you may not be allowed to pair your self-issued badge with the state issued ID. Infringement could cost your license.

Finally, If you legally carry a firearm on the job you must also carry any necessary permits. If you are a firearm enthusiast who owns a self-issued "Concealed Carry" badge, leave this at home, especially if you are also carrying a process server badge. Carrying your badge collection on the job is unnecessary and unprofessional.

Firearms and Service of Process

Indeed, many process servers feel that their duties place them at greater risk than they would normally be subject to. In some regulated states the registration or license process allows for the special server to carry a firearm in the service of duty. This seems only fair since the Sheriff and Constable have that right while performing the same duties. In such states and jurisdictions the license or registration process will inform you of the details. In unregulated states the issue falls to your states arms regulations.

There are a few things to consider in regard to firearms. The first is whether or not your state allows for concealed or open carry of a firearm. If you are already licensed to carry a firearm you will probably choose to do so in the service of process. There is nothing inherently wrong with this but there are some considerations. There are restrictions on firearms on government property and increasingly more private businesses. It may be a felony to accidentally carry your weapon into the local court-house parking lot. In addition, the attorneys who hire you may, or may not, have an issue with it, so concealed carry is preferable.

If you do not currently carry a firearm, you may question whether you should during your job as a process server. This is a personal decision that should be made with much care. If you have never carried a firearm before you will need to take some basic firearm for self defense classes. Your local chapter of the NRA (National Rifle Association) offers such classes.

If, however, you decide to start carrying a firearm only for your job, you may face some difficulties. As an example in Pennsylvania, a suitable candidate may be licensed to carry for the purpose of self defense. If you intend to carry all the time, your license extends to your job under the provisions of self-defense. However, if you possess a job that <u>requires</u> you to carry a weapon, such as an armed security guard, you must undergo additional training and certification offered by the state just for such purposes.

If carrying a firearm is a consideration, you should visit the NRA web site to learn more about the laws of your state and even become a member. Visit www.NRA.org.

Other Weapons

There are a variety of other defensive weapons available to the general public such as Stun-Guns, TASERs and primitive weapons such as knives, clubs and, of course, martial-arts techniques. Most are regulated, to some degree, by local laws. It is your sole responsibility to determining and meeting the laws of your area.

TASERs and Stun Guns are non-lethal defensive weapons that work by discharging vast amounts of electricity into an attacker. TAZERS and Stun-guns are not the same thing. A Stun-gun requires extended personal contact with an individual for several seconds in order to be effective. Exactly how long such contact must be maintained depends on body-weight and other factors; all of which make the stun-gun a questionable line of defense for most people. TASERs, on the other hand, fire two electrodes through the air which penetrate the clothing of an individual and maintain contact from a distance of up to 15 feet while the electrical charge is administered.

The TASER company now makes a civilian version of the same defensive weapon used in Law Enforcement that may be legal in some states where Stun-guns are restricted.

Projecting a professional image

Recently, a woman made an online public inquiry about being served process. She was approached by an "unshaven and dirty-looking" individual wearing a wrinkled blue delivery uniform with a gold badge hung from the shirt pocket that read "Authorized Process Server". On his belt he wore a Stun-gun and, on his head, a baseball cap with the words "Process Server" printed upon it. This guy looked so ridiculous that the person being served was sincerely uncertain as to whether she had really been served process. It all seemed so "goofy".

This is the worst example of the private process server and he is not the kind of person we want representing our profession. It is important to both your success as a process server and to the free enterprise we now enjoy, that we project a positive and professional image to the public.

Never flaunt false authority. Never display your weapons unless the law requires it. And don't go around looking like Cop-Wannabee.

Chapter VI
The Business of Process Service

Throughout this book we have made references to a variety of business models that exist in the Process Service industry. Generally, there are two kinds of Process Servers; officials, such as Sheriffs and Constables, and Private Servers, (Specials) who may or may not be licensed.

Within the private sector there are essentially two ways to work as a process server. You can become an employee of an existing firm or you can strike out on your own. There are advantages and disadvantages to both. Working for an established firm will help you to learn the nuances of the field and may offer steady income. In addition you will learn of potential clients to target later; those of your past employer. This is not dishonest. It's business. If your former employer is providing their clients with great service then they have nothing to worry about. If not, their clients may be interested in trying out alternative services.

The disadvantage of working for another firm is that, as an employee or subcontractor, your earnings per-serve are limited. The old catch-twenty-two is that you need the volume of work that a big broker can provide without the broker getting its share of your profits. However, if you consider this part of your training and experience it is well worth it.

The average typical serve is worth $40-$50.00 Brokers tend to retain at least two thirds, passing along only $10-$15.00 to the server who actually executes the service. In addition, there are often penalties involved. If you don't make service you usually don't get paid; even though you did the leg-work. Some companies actually penalize servers who file non-est by docking their pay on previously executed serves!

Again, the trade-off is that you may run 10-20 papers per day working for a big company and you could make as much as $100.00 for 10 serves. But you usually need to deduct your own fuel costs which, in the current economy, can represent as much as 25% of you daily wages. If you had enough business coming your way as an independent server you could have made $500.00 on the same 10 serves. The problem is: How to scrape up the volume of business you need to justify self-employment?

If you live in a regulated state there may be a list of approved servers published by the court system which will at least get your name onto the desk of every attorney in your jurisdiction. This is a huge benefit of regulated states. But this, in itself, will seldom be enough. You still have to promote your business.

Soliciting Business

The fist place to go is to your local law firms. It is best to start with the smaller, one or two attorney firms. They tend to be easier to approach and you are more likely to be heard. If you have ever hired an attorney in the past you may want to start with them. Explain that you are a former client and that you were very happy with their services. As a result you thought of them first when you decided to seek new clients. A formal letter, written on letterhead, is a good first step in making contact with very small firms, particularly if you are a former client.

For immediate credibility, your web-site, advertisements and letter of introduction should list three points.

- You represent a Corporation, LLC, LLP or other legally established company.

- You are Licensed and Bonded.

- You are a Notary Public (in addition to being a Process Server)

The same techniques may be applied to larger firms; however, your introduction letter will have less overall effect if you attempt to contact the attorneys directly. When dealing with big law firms you should always address your introduction letter to the office manager. It is he or she who most likely decides who handles the process for the firm. Before you send your letter call the office and ask for the name of the office manager. Send the letter directly to their attention.

In addition to attorneys there are other places to solicit business. These include:

- Legal Clinics.
- Collection agencies; tend to be easier to strike a deal.
- Banks; particularly local independents.
- Auto dealerships that self-finance. They do allot of suing.
- Business owners and landlords.
- Citizens; as a service to small claims court. (where applicable)
- Try running a classified or print ad in your local newspaper. You may catch the attention of all of the above.

Offering free services

Some of the Process Server "training courses" out there suggest you offer free services to a potential client. This is your decision to make but it probably will hurt more than it helps. People don't value what comes free or cheap. Offering some "free serves" can devalue your worth in the eyes of a potential client. In addition, "free" is probably not much incentive for your client because attorneys pass along the costs of service to their clients. Saving $50.00 is probably not much of an incentive for an attorney who makes thousands of dollars on a case. Rather than undersell your services, promote your value by emphasizing what you offer that your competitor does not. For example, same-day service, special diligence, no upfront fees, monthly billing, on-line case reporting and tracking etc.

Incorporate!

Before starting to promote your business you need to establish it. The least desirable resource for an attorney to use is an unincorporated, uninsured individual. Put simply, you have no credibility. Working as a self-employed individual is risky to both you and your clients. Consider incorporating your business as a Limited Liability Company (LLC) or Limited Liability Partnership (LLP) if indeed you have a partner. A partner can be a spouse or other relative. Either way, you will instantly reap the benefits of business credibility and you will be able to establish business credit for your company. Remember, every time you need an attorney you have an opportunity to make a potential business contact. There are a variety of do-it-yourself and Internet-based incorporation services available to you, but making contact with a local attorney may be your best chance to promote your business.

Insurance

Once you are incorporated, seek business liability insurance for a minimum of 2 million dollars aggregate coverage. This is not as expensive as it sounds and it will be boon when you can say that you represent an insured LLC. This demands far more respect amongst business professionals than just being some guy who wants to get paid to jockey paper.

Bond

In addition to insurance it is best practice to obtain a professional bond. A Bond protects the attorney who hires you from errors and omissions on your part. It does not protect you. (that's what insurance is for) Being licensed AND bonded is attractive to potential clients. Many process servers have been in operation for many years without insurance or bond. Mentioning your insured and bonded status may serve as a wake-up call to potential clients who have never considered the importance of using only insured and bonded servers. If you are less of a risk than your competition, you may "steal" a client.

Bonding may be a requirement in regulated states. Most firms that bond *Notaries Public* also have bonds for Process Servers.

Once you have your company established you will have long settled on a name. A name can go a long way in this business. Most big companies have authoritative sounding names like "Keystone Procedural", "National Process Service Agency" or "Federal Process Service", etc. Place great care into the naming of your business. Just don't make it hard to remember or spell.

Once you have your corporate name approval it is time to get some letterhead, envelopes, business cards and a web site. In these days of impersonal fax and email communications a professional-quality letterhead goes a long way. When you send letters to potential clients you should use quality letterhead with matching envelopes. Contrary to traditional logic, a neatly hand-written address on a professionally printed envelope will grab attention better than a computer printed address label; the distinctive mark of junk-mail.

A web-site is a necessity. One area where it is not hard for newcomers to make an impact is a good web-site. Have you seen the web sites of other process servers out there? They're not pretty. A web-site that goes above and beyond is the easiest way to grab the attention of potential clients as they surf the web. If you can afford it, pay a professional to design your site; that is unless you are particularly savvy with web design.

Take care when choosing a Domain name. This is the name and address of your web site; those words ending in ".com." Preferably, the Domain should include your business name. For example; KeystoneProcedural.com. If your preferred domain name is already taken by someone else you should not accept the alternative .net, .info or .org or other options because, chances are, anyone searching your name will search for the .com and you will loose business to them. Choose another name and get the .com designation.

Professional Associations

There are a variety of professional associations that can help you promote and expand your business. The most prominent specifically for Process Servers is NAPPS; The *National Association of Professional Process Servers*. You might think this would be the first organization you should join, but it is not. While you are building your business you have better options that are more likely to help you gain a return on your investment. Besides, you must be in business for at least two years and provide letters of recommendation in order to become a NAPPS member. So in the mean time, you should focus on establishing yourself. Later, once you are established, you can go back and explore NAPPS membership.

When considering any kind of membership your first question should always be; "what do they offer me?" If you do not feel that the cost of membership will benefit you in the short to mid-term you should stick with options that will help you to grow your business.

Contact members of an association before joining. Ask them whether they think membership would benefit you as a newcomer to the industry. If an organization hides its membership list for "members-only", they probably are not worth joining. Chances are they have few, if any, real members and are really trying to sell you a bag of goods.

Become a member of your local Chamber of Commerce. If your Chamber has specific categories of membership, be sure to register for the Legal Services category. This will help you connect with local attorneys and paralegals.

Some Sheriff's and Constables associations have a category of membership for non-law enforcement support. This may entitle your business to a listing in a member's directory and participation in formal meetings where you may network. The cost of associate membership is often among the lowest of all the professional associations you could join.

Similarly, Paralegal Associations sometimes have an Associate category of membership that will help you to network with local Paralegals. This is important because the Paralegal often serves as the point of communication between attorneys and servers. In fact, in many law offices, paralegals are often responsible for doling out service of process for their firm. Even if your local paralegal association does not have an Associate membership they may have a Student membership category. Have you thought about becoming a Paralegal? In many cases you can gain Paralegal association membership by entering an approved Paralegal course; many of which are self-study at home! The information gained would be invaluable and the connections you will make through association, would be priceless. It is not necessary to earn a degree to become a Paralegal. Legalstudies.com offers nationally recognized certificate courses through local colleges and universities across the United States. The home-study courses cost little more than $1000.00

NRA Business Alliance

If you are a firearms enthusiast consider becoming an NRA member; if you are not already. The NRA has a special form of membership called the *NRA Business Alliance*. This category of membership for business entities is a great way to network with other enthusiasts and promote your business. The Business Alliance publishes a regular members list that may be referenced by other members (including potential clients) who may give preference to fellow members.

Become a Notary Public!

The best way to be successful as a process server and set yourself apart from the competition is to supplement your repertoire with a variety of related skills and qualifications. The most valuable and easiest to obtain is to become a Notary Public. The duties of a Notary often overlap with those of a process server and doing business as one can generate leads for doing business as the other. It is very common for Notaries Public to do side-work as Process servers and visa versa. This is because aspects of the two professions compliment one another. In states which do not license process servers, being a Notary Public can provide you with the creditability you will need to generate new clients.

Rules and commission requirements regarding Notaries Public vary from state to state. However, one prerequisite that is universal requires Notaries to be of good character and have a history as upstanding citizenship. This, combined with professional training, has made Notaries valued and respected professionals.

As a Process Server you are going to make a trip to see a Notary for Every Service you make. While you will never be allowed to notarize your own affidavits, if you are part of a partnership or manage a small staff of servers your ability to notarize documents served by members of your company can save you thousands of dollars per year. If your partner or spouse becomes a Notary than you have access to in-house Notary services!

The benefits of being a Notary include:

- Access to in-house Notary services. (if you have at least two Notaries in your company)
- Notary and Process Services go hand in hand. One can lead to opportunities in the other.
- Your business card and letter of introduction will reflect immediate credibility when you can say that you are duly appointed Notary Public. A potential client may like the idea of a one-stop source for their Notary and Process Service Needs.
- Opportunities to reap the benefits of side-work as a mobile Notary and break into the lucrative Notary Signing Agent industry.

Support Services

There are a variety of computer software designed to manage your case files. One example is Process Servers Toolbox. (www.dbsinfo.com) which allows process servers to manage their cases from the field (via Internet) and allows your clients to track the status of their orders on-line. This feature is a great incentive to entice clients to use your services, especially if their existing service does not offer on-line tracking and updates.

Specialties and sidelines

Notary Public

As previously stated, becoming a Notary opens doors to opportunities an sidelines that go hand-in-hand with Process Service. Make sure you also join your local Notary Association.

Special Diligence

Many servers have made a business of handling only hard-to-serve cases. This specialty generally starts with skip-tracing and may include lots of hours conducting research, surveillance and leg-work. This is a good specialty for experienced process servers or private investigators who sideline in process service. Most servers charge by the hour at rates comparable to those of a private investigator.

Same-day service

Same day service is a good specialty for either large metropolitan areas or very small rural areas. You can generally charge at least twice the regular fee for same day service. However, some processes don't lend well to same-day service. This specialty applies best to serve-or-post and service at a business.

Locate & Skip trace

As long as it is in the duty of service of process you can offer skip-trace as an add-on to your regular service offerings. The rate for a typical trace should be just below the typical rates charged by private investigators.

Address verification

Sometimes attorneys and collection agencies need to verify an address of a debtor or defendant. In most cases this simply involves confirmation of abode by personal witness. Whether or not you are allowed to perform address verification depends largely on whether the practice falls within the jurisdiction of private investigation; per your local laws.

Judgment recovery

When a plaintiff wins an award by court order they usually have no idea how to enforce it; and the courts generally don't offer much help. Very often the debtor disappears leaving the creditor unable to collect. This provides a lucrative opportunity for a knowledgeable judgment recovery agent who can put his detective skills to use in locating the debtor and executing a variety of actions, such as wage garnishment or liens on real property, to enforce the judgment. This requires special knowledge on the part of the recovery agent. A variety of courses and books are available on the subject. Note: This is most lucrative in states that allow wage garnishment and which do not grant exemptions to debtors. For example, in Pennsylvania there is no wage garnishment and in Florida and California exemption options make it more difficult to enforce judgments than in other states. Know the rules of civil procedure in your state before you decide to work in this field. Keep in mind that you will probably need to appear in court for each case you take on; therefore, you should only take on cases in your immediate vicinity.

Court filing

Court filing used to be a lucrative sideline for process servers. These days electronic court-filing has all but eliminated the need for manual filing in most states and jurisdictions.

Rules to live by

Some important notes.

Service in court

Generally you may not serve someone while they are engaged in court. Some attorneys will send you to serve an individual in transit to court for an unrelated matter. You may make service as they enter the courthouse or upon exit, but not in the courtroom.

Holy Time

Remember; in some states it is illegal to serve on Sundays or Saturdays when the individual being served counts Saturday as a holiday. (Judaism and Islam) Know your rules and the rules of other states when handling foreign paper.

Foreign Paper

As your business grows you may be contacted from attorneys in other states to make service on a person now residing in your state. It is important to remember that when making service on behalf of an out-of-state jurisdiction you must serve according to the rules of the state in which the process originates. In States where only the Sheriff or Deputy may make service you must be appointed or deputized to serve their process in your own state. Always check the rules of the jurisdiction of origin and never hesitate to call the issuing court or attorney for further information. After all it's their case and they want it done right.

Answers for self-quiz on page 43.

1. F
2. T
3. F
4. T
5. F
6. F
7. F
8. F
9. F
10. F

Made in the USA
Lexington, KY
31 October 2011